CULTURE
in the Kitchen

FOODS OF
West Africa

By Ethan Y. Garten

Gareth Stevens
Publishing

Please visit our website, www.garethstevens.com. For a free color catalog of all our high-quality books, call toll free 1-800-542-2595 or fax 1-877-542-2596.

Library of Congress Cataloging-in-Publication Data

Garten, Ethan Y.
Foods of West Africa / Ethan Y. Garten.
    p. cm. — (Culture in the kitchen)
Includes bibliographical references and index.
ISBN 978-1-4339-5724-6 (pbk.)
ISBN 978-1-4339-5725-3 (6-pack)
ISBN 978-1-4339-5722-2 (library binding)
   1. Cooking, West African—Juvenile literature. 2. Food habits—Africa, West—Juvenile literature. 3. Food—Africa, West—Juvenile literature. 4. Diet—Africa, West—Juvenile literature. 5. Africa, West—Social life and customs—Juvenile literature. I. Title.
TX725.W47G37 2012
394.1'20966—dc22

2010053250

First Edition

Published in 2012 by
Gareth Stevens Publishing
111 East 14th Street, Suite 349
New York, NY 10003

Designer: Daniel Hosek
Editor: Therese Shea

Photo credits: Cover, p. 1 Travel Ink/Gallo Images/Getty Images; pp. 5, 6, 8, 12, 14, 21 Shutterstock.com; p. 7 Angus McBride/The Bridgeman Art Library/Getty Images; p. 9 Peeter Viisimaa/Vetta/Getty Images; p. 11 Lynn Johnson/National Geographic/Getty Images; p. 13 Steve Gorton/Dorling Kindersley/Getty Images; p. 15 Heinrich van den Berg/Gallo Images/Getty Images; p. 17 Nico Tondini/Robert Harding World Imagery/Getty Images; p. 19 Seyllou/AFP/Getty Images.

Printed in the United States of America

CPSIA compliance information: Batch #CS11GS: For further information contact Gareth Stevens, New York, New York at 1-800-542-2595.

Contents

Words in the glossary appear in **bold** type the first time they are used in the text.

The Countries of West Africa

The countries of west Africa include Benin, Burkina Faso, Cameroon, Cape Verde, Chad, Gambia, Ghana, Guinea, Guinea-Bissau, Ivory Coast, Liberia, Mali, Mauritania, Niger, Nigeria, Saint Helena, Senegal, Sierra Leone, Togo, and Western Sahara.

West Africa's northern border runs through the Sahara Desert. The Atlantic Ocean is to the west. West Africa has grasslands and rainforests, too. Despite the different **regions**, west Africans share a love of certain foods and dishes. The history of west African **cuisine** can be traced back hundreds of years.

Western
Sahara

Cape
Verde

Mauritania

Mali

Niger

Chad

Senegal

Gambia

Guinea

Burkina
Faso

Guinea-
Bissau

Ivory
Coast

Nigeria

Sierra
Leone

Togo

Cameroon

Liberia

Benin

Ghana

Saint Helena

In addition to the countries on mainland Africa,
many people include the islands of Cape
Verde and Saint Helena as part of west Africa.

History of Trade

Slavery shaped the history of west Africa. The slave trade even affected its cuisine. Arabs first arrived in Africa over 2,000 years ago. They traded spices, **herbs**, and salt to Africans in return for gold, ivory, and slaves.

Later, Europeans sailed to west Africa. In return for slaves, they offered plants from the Americas such as peanuts, plantains, chili peppers, and corn. The European traders took African crops to the Americas. Many became part of the American South's cuisine, including sesame seeds, **okra**, and black-eyed peas.

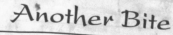

Another Bite

The thick stew called gumbo gets its name from the Ibo language spoken in Nigeria. *Gomba* means "okra," which is an ingredient in gumbo.

Many African slaves were people who had been captured in war, criminals, or those who owed money.

One Meal, One Pot

Today, most west Africans eat one large meal a day, usually in the evening. It's a time for families, neighbors, and friends to sit down and share news. Commonly, men sit separately from women.

The evening meal is cooked in one pot. It's mostly made up of vegetables such as corn, **cassavas**, or yams. Rice and other grains, such as millet, may be added. People either scoop up the food with their fingers or use pieces of bread.

plantains

Another Bite

A common west African food is the plantain, which is a greenish-yellow fruit that looks like a banana. Plantains can be fried, boiled, baked, or grilled. They're also made into flour.

West Africans use their right hand to bring food to their mouth. Using the left hand is thought to be rude.

9

Meat and Fish

Though small bits of meat may be included in west African meals, it's often left out. West Africans who live in cities tend to eat more meat, but many others can't get it. Still others can't afford meat.

Africans who raise livestock most often use them for milk and cheese, not for meat. However, meals for special **celebrations** may include meat such as chicken, goat, lamb, or beef. Africans who live near the coast or rivers eat fish when they can.

Another Bite

West African farmers use cows' milk to make a sour food that's much like yogurt.

This photo shows a Fulani boy tending cattle in Nigeria. The Fulani are a traveling people who trade and herd animals.

Spice and Oil

Dishes made mostly of root vegetables don't have a lot of **flavor**. That's why spices are so important to west Africans. The spice called grains of paradise comes from the seeds of the melegueta pepper. It tastes a bit like black pepper and ginger combined.

Another important ingredient of west African cuisine is palm oil. It's made from the fruit of palm trees. Palm oil gives food a reddish color. It's used the way butter and oil are used in other cuisines.

palm oil

palm seeds

Kola nuts, shown here as a powder, are an important part of west African cuisine. Grains of paradise are shown at the bottom of the page.

ot Peppers in a Hot Land

Chili peppers are perhaps the most important ingredient in west African cooking. Besides adding flavor to a dish, chili peppers offer another interesting benefit. Eating hot peppers makes people sweat. Sweat on the surface of the skin helps cool bodies. Staying cool is important in the extreme heat of west Africa.

Piri-piri means "pepper-pepper" in the African language of Swahili. It's also what many Africans call the bird's-eye chili and others call the African red devil. This pepper is used to make spicy sauces.

scotch bonnet peppers

Bird's-eye chilis, shown here, and scotch bonnets, shown on page 14, are both popular in west Africa.

Fufu

The popular west African dish called fufu (or foo foo) is made of yams, plantains, cassavas, and other vegetables. These are cooked and crushed into a paste. To eat fufu the west African way, a bit of the paste is rolled into a ball. The ball is dipped into a sauce or stew and then eaten. It takes a lot of time to make fufu. The mix must be pounded until it can be swallowed without being chewed.

Another Bite

Quick-cooking fufu is now sold in boxes in west African stores. However, many Africans think it doesn't taste as good as homemade fufu.

Africans who traveled to Caribbean nations continued to make fufu there. This photo shows a Cuban fufu dish.

17

Peanut Stew

Portuguese traders probably brought peanuts to west Africa from South America in the 1560s. By the 1600s, peanuts were growing very successfully. For years, scientists thought they had always grown there.

Today, peanuts are found in many west African dishes. They're **roasted** and eaten as snacks. They're pounded into peanut butter, too. They're also used to make the popular peanut stew. Peanuts, tomatoes, onions, and chili peppers are cooked together in a pot. Sometimes meat is also added.

Here a worker in Senegal shovels a mountain of harvested peanuts.

19

Jollof Rice

Rice is another important crop in Africa. Parts of west Africa get the rain needed to water rice fields. It has been growing in the country now called Mali for more than 2,000 years.

The Wolof people of Senegal and Gambia may have been the first to make jollof, a popular rice dish. Jollof rice is also called *bena-chin*, which in Wolof means "one pot." In a single pot, rice is mixed with meat or fish, tomatoes, onions, and spices.

Another Bite

There are two kinds of rice crops: African and Asian. Asian rice has been replacing African rice on west Africa's farms in recent years.

Recipe:
Sesame Seed Sticks

(Also called *meni-meniyong* in Mali, this dish requires the help of an adult.)

Ingredients:
1 cup sesame seeds
1/4 cup butter
1 cup honey (or sugar)

Directions:

1. Heat the sesame seeds in a pan until they begin to turn brown. Shake the pan during heating so that the seeds don't stick or burn. Let them cool.

2. Heat the butter in a pan, then add the honey. Stir until the mixture begins to turn slightly brown.

3. Pour the sesame seeds into the butter-honey mixture and stir.

4. Pour the seed mixture onto a cookie sheet. When the mixture cools, shape it into sticks. Coat the sticks with more sesame seeds if they're still sticky.

Glossary

cassava: a plant that has large roots that can be eaten

celebration: a time to show happiness for an event through activities such as eating or playing music

cuisine: a style of cooking

flavor: a feature of a food or drink that gives it a special taste

herb: a low-growing plant used to add flavor to food

ingredient: a part of a mixture

okra: a plant that grows in warm places and has green pods that can be eaten

region: a large area of land that has features that make it different from nearby areas of land

roast: to heat a food until it is dry or brown

For More Information

Books

Barr, Gary E. *History and Activities of the West African Kingdoms*. Chicago, IL: Heinemann Library, 2007.

Ekunsanmi, Toye. *What Africans Eat: Traditional Foods and Food Traditions of West Africa*. Denver, CO: Outskirts Press, 2010.

Websites

Africa for Kids

pbskids.org/africa/

Learn more about the lives of children in Africa.

Global Destinations: West Africa

www.globalgourmet.com/destinations/westafrica/

Read more about the foods of the west African nations.

Index